By Donna Barton

To [Melody]
Millie
I call you melody
because you make
me want to sing.

Donna Barton
DB

To order additional copies of this book, contact:
Xlibris Corporation
1-888-795-4274
www.Xlibris.com
Orders@Xlibris.com

יהוה

Yahweh

To Jesus, who gave me my wonderful family:
Mother, Larry, Shona, Curt,

Sheila, JJ, Ashley, and Emma. Special thanks
to my husband Larry, Shona, Sheila,
and Julie.

As parents, it is important to instill in our children a respect and reverence for our Creator. The Jewish people held God in great reverence and taught their children to speak of God with respect. They did this by reading and teaching the Scriptures to the children and by obeying the special rites ordained by God throughout their history.

God's name was regarded with awe. It was not to be spoken or even written without certain rules being followed. For instance, when the name of God was copied into the scriptures by the scribes, a new pen was used and then it was broken and thrown away. These and other strict traditions were followed by the scribes every time they wrote the name down and even then only the consonants YHWH were used. The name of God was never spoken aloud. As a result, we are not sure how God's name is pronounced.

It has been said that the pronunciation of God's name is the sound of breathing. The name of God in Hebrew is the word for breath. God breathed the breath of life into the first living human beings. The spirit of God is in our nostrils and the very breath of God fills our lungs. We share God's breath. Every breath we take is a prayer of praise to the King of Kings.

My prayer is that you can use this praise book to teach your children that God is with them every day as their Creator, Helper, King, LORD, and Everlasting God.

May you never breathe the same again.

Everyone has a name. God has a name too!
His name is so special that we say it every time
we breathe. The first part of God's name is
like taking a breath to blow a bubble.
We breathe in… "Yah" like a whisper.
We breathe out like a whisper…"Weh".
Psalm 150:6 says, "Let everything that has breath
praise the LORD". And that means you and me,
and…

the little bitty worm, the tiny chickadee

The bunnies hiding in the deep green leaves

breathe praises to their creator

The jolly dragonfly, the busy buzzing bee

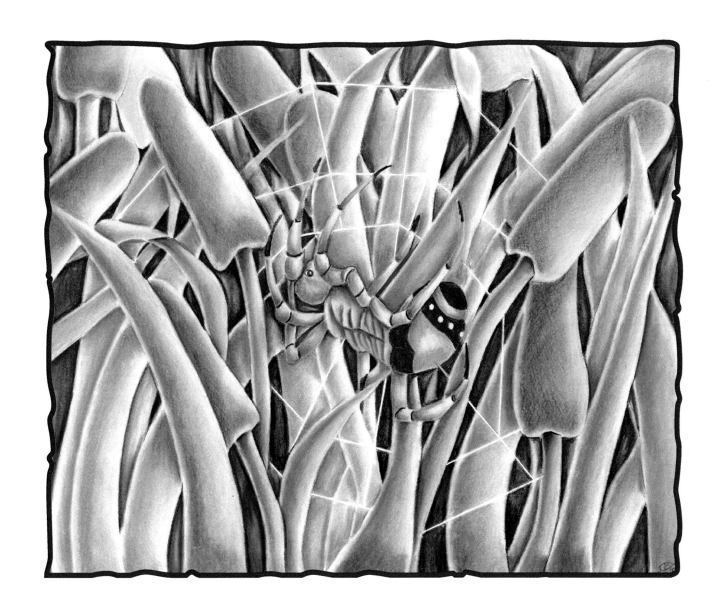

The hairy spider on his web trapeze

Breathe praises to their helper

The grizzly threatens all with awesome
huff and cry

While silent on the plain the giraffe can only sigh

praise to his God

The whale is singing songs in
ocean depths profound

Only God can hear the strange sweet sound

Praising almighty God

In dappled forest glade,
the fawn lies quiet and still

In meadow green and bright,
the babbling brooklet trills

Praises to their King

Creation great and small, together stand amazed

And glorify His name in symphony of praise

Always praising the everlasting King

Children are God's great joy. They are so
sweet and small. And with their every breath,
their hearts will loudly call

Yahweh Yahweh Yahweh

Let everything that has breath praise the LORD.
Psalm 150:6

Edwards Brothers Malloy
Thorofare, NJ USA
October 24, 2012